This Planner Belongs to:

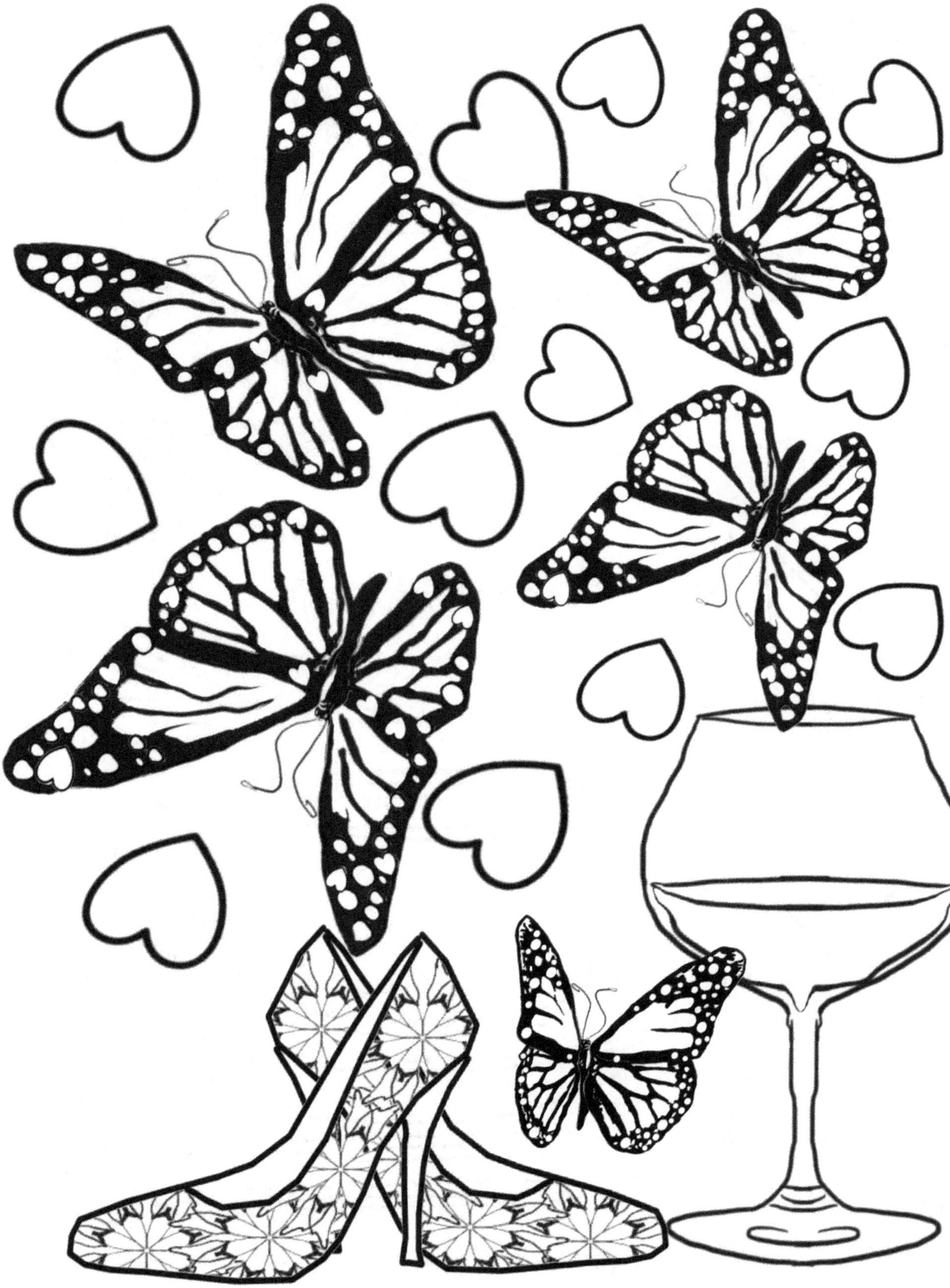

Fuck Me ♡ Fuck Me ♡ Fuck Me

Mr. and Mrs :

_____

Wedding Date :

_____

Maybe
Swearing
Will Help

Fuck Me ♡ Fuck Me ♡

3

FML ♡ WTF ♡ LMAO ♡ BFD ♡ STFU

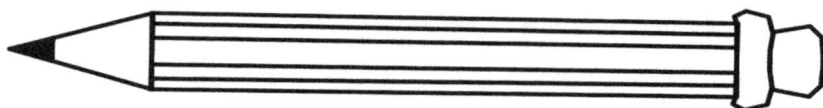

Fuck Me!
My Wedding Planner

GD

GTFO

FYFI

SFF

GD

GTFO

FYFI

SFF

FML ♡ WTF ♡ LMAO ♡ BFD ♡ STFU

Shit, Let's Get Going!

Hell, Looking Good!

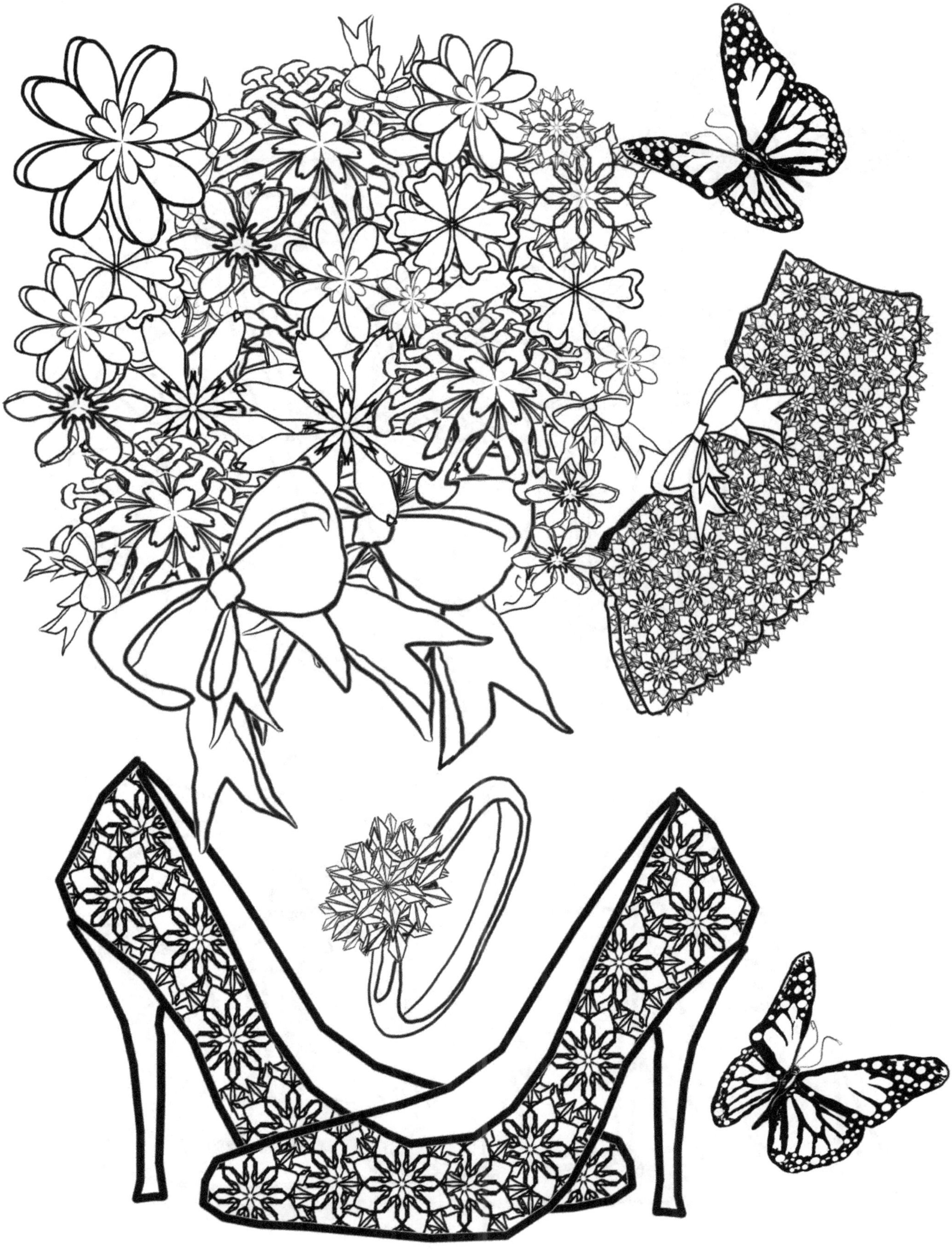

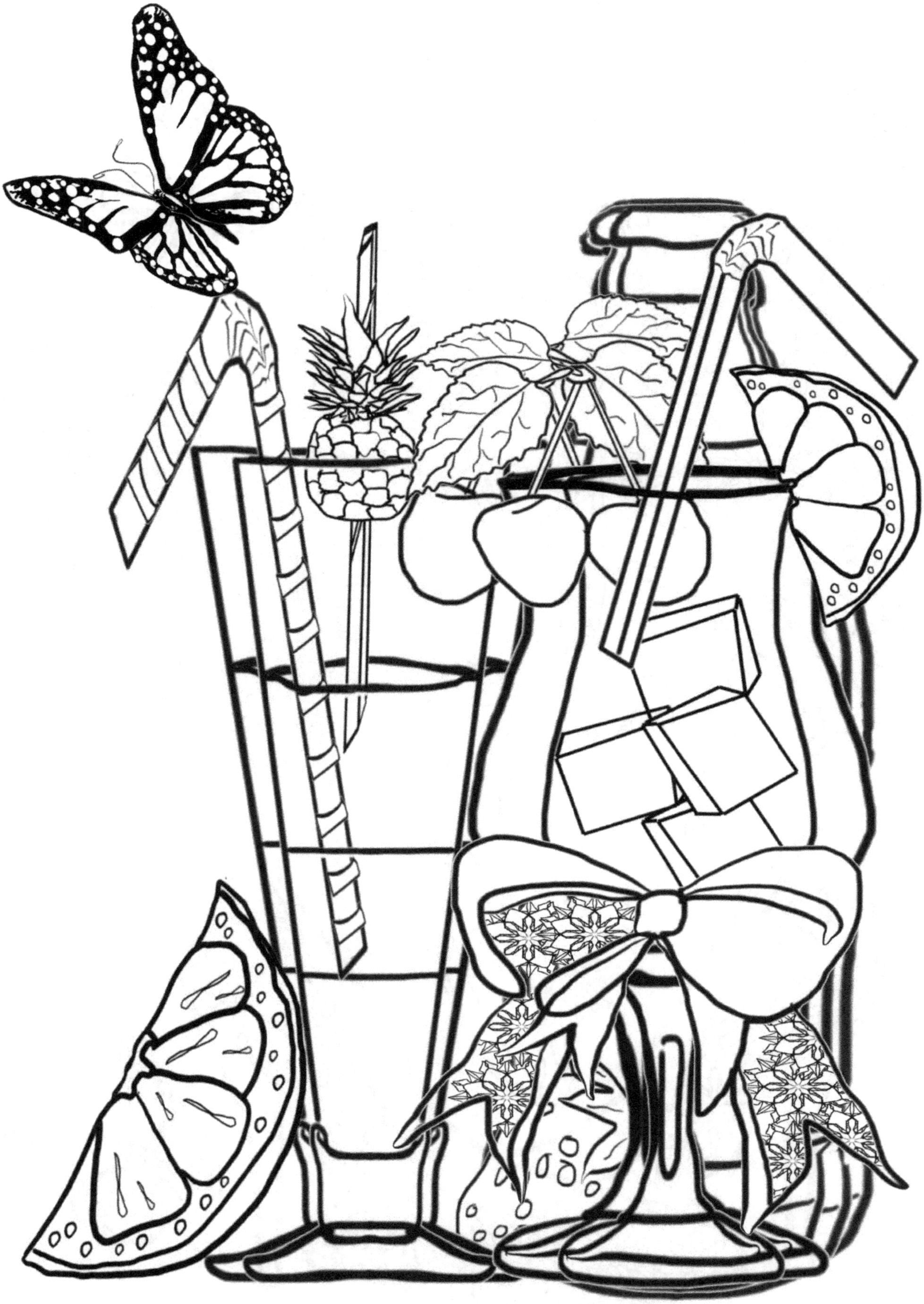

Wine and Beer Tracker

Weekly

Date:___

Fuck Me!

Wine, Love Red and Fucking Dry

Chips

CLASSIC

ALE

Shit, I Love Junk Food

Thank You So Much Have a Great Week

Merlot

White

Bitch Bitch Bitch Bitch Bitch Bitch Bitch Bitch

Wedding Planning
CheckList

✓

- Set The Date\ Time
- Wedding Planner
- Wedding Venue
- Reception Venue
- Guest List
- Officiant
- Catering Sample Food
- Florist

- Invitations
- DJ Services/ Band
- Rentals
- Wedding Cake
- Bridle Dress
- Bridle Attire
- Bridle Jewelry
- Something Old/ Borrowed ?

Shit, Have to Invite Beth, Fuck!

14

Wedding Planning Checklist ✓

- Groom's Tuxedo
- Groom's Attire
- Bridesmaids Attire
- Groomsmen Attire
- Flower Girl Attire
- Ring Boy Attire
- Pick Colour Theme
- Overall Vision

- Wedding Registry
- Email Addresses
- Tour Venues
- Hair / Makeup
- Wedding License
- Invitation List
- Wedding Website
- Any Permits ?

Look At Me. Hell. I am getting Married

Wedding Planning Checklist

- ❤ Wedding Crew Wedding Timeline
- ❤ Break in Wedding Shoes
- ❤ Research Wedding (Required Insurance)
- ❤ Decide on Weather Plan
- ❤ Track RSVPs/ __Non- Repliers__
- ❤ Final Guest Count
- ❤ Organize Guest Book
- ❤ Order Wedding Programs

- ❤ Bachelorette Party Plans ?
- ❤ Bachelor Party Plans ?
- ❤ Meet with Photographer
- ❤ Practice Vows
- ❤ Confirm Bouquets Boutonniere's
- ❤ Pay Wedding Bills
- ❤ Finalize Budget
- ❤ _Finalize Everything_

16

Wedding Planning
3 Month Checklist

- Write Your Vows
- Dress Fittings
- Tuxedos Alterations
- Dress Alterations
- Check On Florist
- Choose Your Music
- Schedule Pictures
- Send Wedding Invitations

- Wedding Crew Gifts
- Venue Table Decor
- Music Playlist
- Rehearsal Dinner
- Wedding Bands
- Book Flights/Transportion
- Seating Order
- Confirm Hotel Reservations

Do I Want To Take His Last Name?
Shit Yes

Wedding Day
CheckList

- Have a Good Night Sleep
- Healthy Breakfast
- Check-in With Wedding Planner
- Brides Crew Get Together
- Manicure & Pedicure
- Mint or Mouthwash
- Band-aids
- Hydrate

- Pack a Night & Evening Bag
- Hair / Makeup Accessories
- Tylenol
- Hand Sanitizer
- Antacids
- Comfortable Shoes
- Stain Remover Pen
- Relax and Enjoy Your Day

Fuck, I Getting Married Today!
Love it!

18

Wedding Planning

If You are Eloping

- ♡ Choose Location
- ♡ Choose a Date/ Time
- ♡ Wedding Package
- ♡ Decide On Your Witnesses
- ♡ Book Travel Arrangements
- ♡ Apply for Marriage License/Permit
- ♡ Set a Budget
- ♡ Hair/ Makeup Suppliers

- ♡ Wedding Gown
- ♡ Grooms Attire
- ♡ Lingerie/ Garter
- ♡ Put Deposit Down
- ♡ Rings
- ♡ Hire Photographer
- ♡ Timeline
- ♡ Ceremony Outline

Eloping, Hell Yes!

19

Wedding Planning

If You are Eloping

- Research Your Wedding Packages
- Write Wedding Vows
- Confirm Time/ Dates with Witnesses
- Manicure/ Pedicure
- Dress Fitting
- Weather Backup Plans
- Pay Wedding Bills
- Plan Fun Activities

- Break in Shoes
- Hair/Makeup Trial Run
- Send Invites?
- Food/Drink
- Florals
- Bug Spray Sunscreen
- Make it Simple
- *Get Married*

ROFAPMS

WTFG

 # Notes
Random Fucking Thoughts

Date: _____

Bitch Meter

21

Random Fucking Thoughts

Date: _____

Bitch Meter

Water Water Water Water Water Water Water Water Water

Water Water Water Water Water Water Water Water Water

Notes
Random Fucking Thoughts

Date: _____

Bitch Meter

23

Wedding Day
Times

Ceremony  _____

Cocktail Hour  _____

First Dance  _____

Dinner _____

Speeches _____

Cake Cutting _____

Let's Get the
Fuck Out of here _____

24

My Big Fucking Scribble

Theme Ideas

Colour Ideas

27

Venue Ideas

28

Music Ideas

Reception Ideas

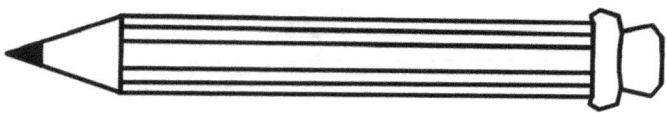

Catering Ideas

Notes
Random Fucking Thoughts

Date: _____

Bitch Meter

Water Water Water Water Water Water Water Water Water

Water Water Water Water Water Water Water Water Water

Notes
Random Fucking Thoughts

Bitch Meter

Notes

Random Fucking Thoughts

Date: _____

Bitch Meter

Water Water Water Water Water Water Water Water Water

Water Water Water Water Water Water Water Water Water

34

Notes
Random Fucking Thoughts

Date: _____

Bitch Meter

35

Colour Palette Ideas

Combination 1

Combination 2

Combination 3

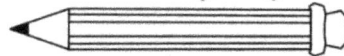

Colour WTF Palette Ideas

Combination 4

Combination 5

Combination 6

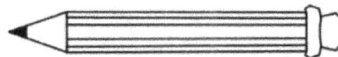

Colour FML Palette Ideas

Combination 7

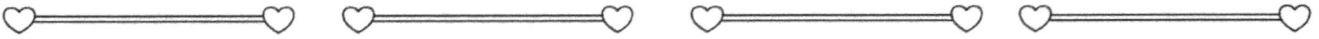

Combination 8

Combination 9

38

Notes

Random Fucking Thoughts

Date: _____

Bitch Meter

♡ Colour & Styles Ideas

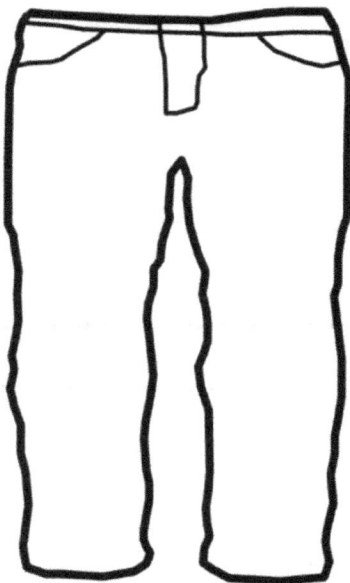

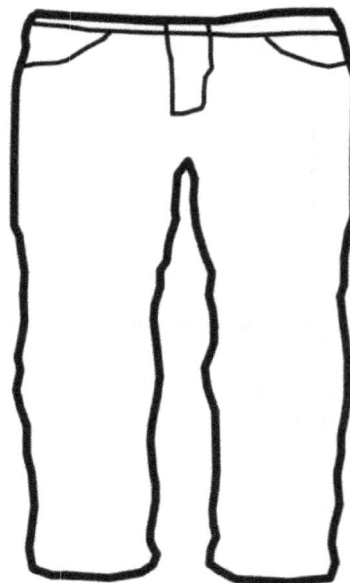

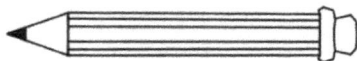

Notes
Colour & Styles

Styles Ideas

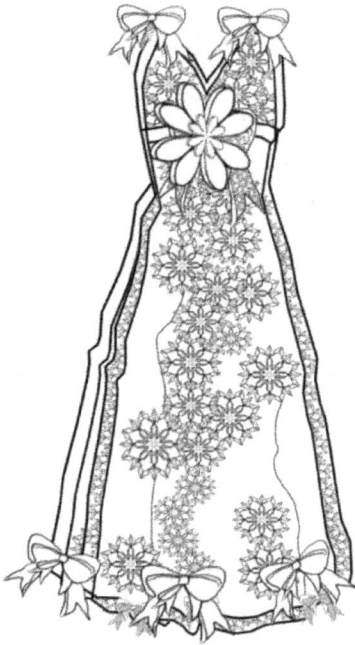

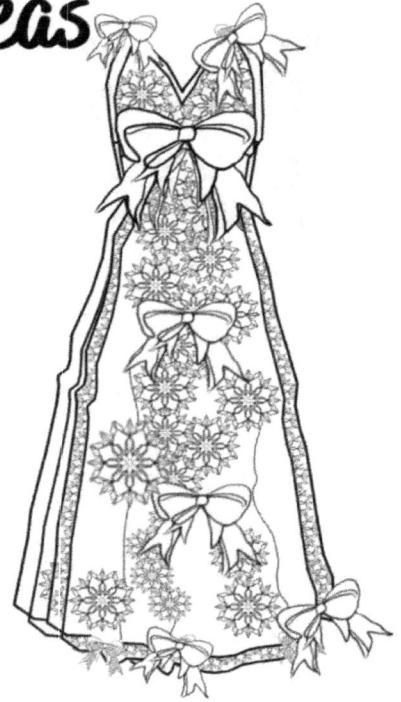

42

Notes
Styles & Ideas

Liquor & Wine Ideas

Merlot

White

ALE

LAGER

Malibu

Shit faced, Yes!

Notes
Liquor and Wine List

Catering Ideas

Premium
100%
Orange Juice

No Sugar Added

Chip

CLASSIC

Peps

Notes
Catering

Notes
Random Fucking Thoughts

Date: _____

Bitch Meter

Water Water Water Water Water Water Water Water Water

Water Water Water Water Water Water Water Water Water

Notes

Random Fucking Thoughts

Date: _____

Bitch Meter

49

Notes

Random Fucking Thoughts

Date: _____

Bitch Meter

Water Water Water Water Water Water Water Water Water

Water Water Water Water Water Water Water Water Water

Notes
Random Fucking Thoughts

Date: _____

Bitch Meter

Stay Hydrated

Date:_____

I LoveWater, Drink up Bitch

52

Stay Hydrated

    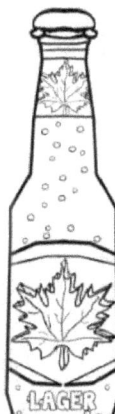  

FML

Piss Off

53

Stay Hydrated

Date: _____

I Love Water, Drink up Bitch

Stay Hydrated

Date:

 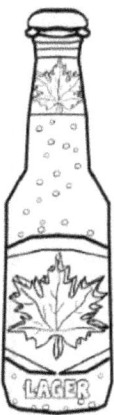 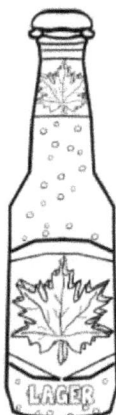    

FML   Piss Off

Notes
Random Fucking Thoughts

Bitch Meter

Notes
Random Fucking Thoughts

Date:

Bitch Meter

Notes

Random Fucking Thoughts

Date:

Bitch Meter

Water Water Water Water Water Water Water Water Water

Water Water Water Water Water Water Water Water Water

Notes
Random Fucking Thoughts

Date:_____

Bitch Meter

Notes

Random Fucking Thoughts

Bitch Meter

Water Water Water Water Water Water Water Water Water

Water Water Water Water Water Water Water Water Water

Notes
Random Fucking Thoughts

Date: _____

Bitch Meter

61

Notes

Random Fucking Thoughts

Date: ———

Bitch Meter

Water Water Water Water Water Water Water Water Water

Water Water Water Water Water Water Water Water Water

Random Fucking Thoughts

Date:———

Bitch Meter

Date: _____

Guest List

Fuck, I am So Excited!

Guest	Cell/Phone	Address	Email

Guest List
Fuck, I am So Excited!

Guest	Cell/Phone	Address	Email

Guest List
Fuck, I am so Excited!

Guest	Cell/Phone	Address	Email

Date:

Date:_____

Guest List
Fuck, I am so Excited!

Guest	Cell/Phone	Address	Email

Guest List

Fuck, I am so Excited!

Date: _____

Guest	Cell/Phone	Address	Email

Guest List
Fuck, I am so Excited!

Date: _____

Guest	Cell/Phone	Address	Email

Date: _____

Guest List
Fuck, I am So Excited!

Guest	Cell/Phone	Address	Email

Date:———

Guest List
Fuck, I am So Excited!

Guest	Cell/Phone	Address	Email

Notes

Random Fucking Thoughts

Date:

Bitch Meter

Water Water Water Water Water Water Water Water Water

Water Water Water Water Water Water Water Water Water

Notes
Random Fucking Thoughts

Date: _____

Bitch Meter

Notes
Random Fucking Thoughts

Date: _____

Bitch Meter

Water Water Water Water Water Water Water Water Water

Water Water Water Water Water Water Water Water Water

Notes

Random Fucking Thoughts

Date:——

Bitch Meter

75

Notes
Random Fucking Thoughts

Date: _____

Bitch Meter

Random Fucking Thoughts

Date: _____

Bitch Meter

☆☆☆☆☆

Date: _____

Wedding Supplier List

Supplier	Cell/Phone	Address	Email

Date: _____

Wedding Supplier List

Supplier	Cell/Phone	Address	Email

Wedding Supplier List

Date: _____

Supplier	Cell/Phone	Address	Email

Wedding Supplier List

Date: _____

Supplier	Cell/Phone	Address	Email

Wedding Supplier List

Date: _____

Supplier	Cell/Phone	Address	Email

Wedding Supplier List

Date: _____

Supplier	Cell/Phone	Address	Email

Wedding Supplier List

Date: _____

Supplier	Cell/Phone	Address	Email

Date: _____

Wedding Supplier List

Supplier	Cell/Phone	Address	Email

85

Date: _____

Wedding Supplier List

Supplier	Cell/Phone	Address	Email

Wedding Supplier List

Date: _____

Supplier	Cell/Phone	Address	Email

Wedding Supplier List

Date: _____

Supplier	Cell/Phone	Address	Email

Wedding Supplier List

Date: _____

Supplier	Cell/Phone	Address	Email

Notes

Random Fucking Thoughts

Date: ———

Bitch Meter

Water Water Water Water Water Water Water Water Water

Water Water Water Water Water Water Water Water Water

Random Fucking Thoughts

Date: _____

Bitch Meter

Notes
Random Fucking Thoughts

Date: _____

Bitch Meter

Notes
Random Fucking Thoughts

Date: _____

Bitch Meter

Budget

Date: _____

Item	Budget	Cost	Deposit	Balance

Stick to a Budget, Bitch!

Total _____

Budget

Date: _____

S S M T W T F

Item	Budget	Cost	Deposit	Balance

Stick to a Budget, Bitch!

Total _____

95

Budget

Date: _____

Item	Budget	Cost	Deposit	Balance

Stick to a Budget, Bitch!

Total _____

96

Budget

Date: _____

S S M T W T F

Item	Budget	Cost	Deposit	Balance

Stick to a Budget, Bitch!

Total _____

97

Budget

Date: _____

S S M T W T F

Item	Budget	Cost	Deposit	Balance

Stick to a Budget, Bitch!

Total

_____

Budget

Date: _____

S S M T W T F

Item	Budget	Cost	Deposit	Balance

Stick to a Budget, Bitch!

Total _____

99

Budget

Date: _____

S S M T W T F

Item	Budget	Cost	Deposit	Balance

Stick to a Budget, Bitch!

Total _____

100

Budget

Date: _____

S S M T W T F

Item	Budget	Cost	Deposit	Balance

Stick to a Budget, Bitch!

Total _____

101

Budget

Date: _____

Item	Budget	Cost	Deposit	Balance

Stick to a Budget, Bitch!

Total _____

102

Budget

Date: _____

Item	Budget	Cost	Deposit	Balance

Stick to a Budget, Bitch!

Total _____

103

Budget

Date: _____

Item	Budget	Cost	Deposit	Balance

Stick to a Budget, Bitch!

Total _____

104

Budget

Date: _____

S S M T W T F

Item	Budget	Cost	Deposit	Balance

Stick to a Budget, Bitch!

Total _____

Notes

Random Fucking Thoughts

Date: _____

Bitch Meter

Notes

Date: _____

Random Fucking Thoughts

Bitch Meter

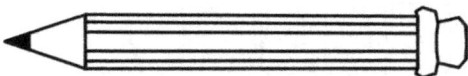

Notes

Random Fucking Thoughts

Date: _____

Bitch Meter

Water Water Water Water Water Water Water Water Water

Water Water Water Water Water Water Water Water Water

Notes
Random Fucking Thoughts

Date: _____

Bitch Meter

Weight Tracker

Date:——

Mon   Tues   Wed   Thur   Fri   Sat   Sun

Weight Loss starts Today

Sweat it Out

No Sweets

Amazing

Don't Quit

Hell, No more Cookies?

You Got This!   Wedding Day

110

Weight Tracker

Date:_____

Mon   Tues   Wed   Thur   Fri   Sat   Sun

Weight Loss starts Today

Sweat it Out

No Sweets

Amazing

Don't Quit

You Got This!

Wedding Day

Hell, No more Cookies?

Weight Tracker

Date: _____

Mon   Tues   Wed   Thur   Fri   Sat   Sun

Weight Loss starts Today

Sweat it Out

No Sweets

Amazing

Don't Quit

You Got This!   Wedding Day

Hell, No more Cookies?

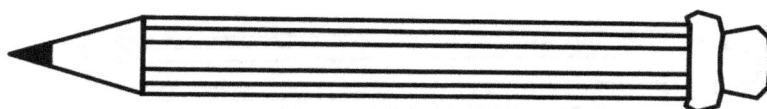

112

Weight Tracker

Date:_____

Mon   Tues   Wed   Thur   Fri   Sat   Sun

Weight Loss starts Today

Sweat it Out

No Sweets

Amazing

Don't Quit

Hell, No more Cookies?

You Got This!   Wedding Day

113

Weight Tracker

Date: _____

Mon   Tues   Wed   Thur   Fri   Sat   Sun

Weight Loss starts Today

Sweat it Out

No Sweets

Amazing

Don't Quit

You Got This!

Wedding Day

Hell, No more Cookies?

114

Weight Tracker

Date: _____

Mon   Tues   Wed   Thur   Fri   Sat   Sun

Weight Loss starts Today

Sweat it Out

No Sweets

Amazing

Don't Quit

You Got This!   Wedding Day

Hell, No more Cookies?

115

Weight Tracker

Mon	Tues	Wed	Thur	Fri	Sat	Sun

Weight Loss starts Today

Sweat it Out

No Sweets

Amazing

Don't Quit

You Got This!

Hell, No more Cookies?

Wedding Day

116

Weight Tracker

Date: _____

Mon   Tues   Wed   Thur   Fri   Sat   Sun

Weight Loss starts Today

Sweat it Out

No Sweets

Amazing

Don't Quit

You Got This!   Wedding Day

Hell, No more Cookies?

117

Weight Tracker

Date: _____

Mon Tues Wed Thur Fri Sat Sun

Weight Loss starts Today

Sweat it Out

No Sweets

Amazing

Don't Quit

Hell, No more Cookies?

You Got This!   Wedding Day

118

Weight Tracker

Mon Tues Wed Thur Fri Sat Sun

Weight Loss starts Today

Sweat it Out

No Sweets

Amazing

Don't Quit

You Got This!   *Wedding Day*

Hell, No more Cookies?

119

Weight Tracker

Date: _____

Mon   Tues   Wed   Thur   Fri   Sat   Sun

Weight Loss starts Today

Sweat it Out

No Sweets

Amazing

Don't Quit

Hell, No more Cookies?

You Got This!   Wedding Day

120

Weight Tracker

Date: _____

Mon   Tues   Wed   Thur   Fri   Sat   Sun

Weight Loss starts Today

Sweat it Out

No Sweets

Amazing

Don't Quit

You Got This!   Wedding Day

Hell, No more Cookies?

Notes

Random Fucking Thoughts

Date: _____

Bitch Meter

122

Notes
Random Fucking Thoughts

Date: _____

Bitch Meter

123

Notes
Random Fucking Thoughts

Date: _____

Bitch Meter

Water Water Water Water Water Water Water Water Water

Water Water Water Water Water Water Water Water Water

124

Notes

Random Fucking Thoughts

Date:_____

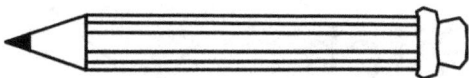

Bitch Meter

125

Stay Hydrated

Date:_____

I LoveWater, Drink up Bitch

126

Stay Hydrated

 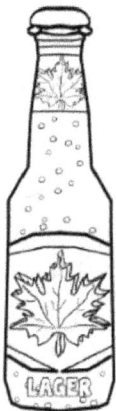 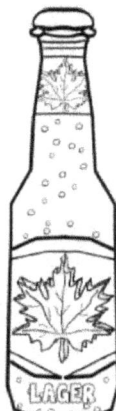    

FML   Piss Off

127

Stay Hydrated

Date:_____

I LoveWater, Drink up Bitch

Stay Hydrated

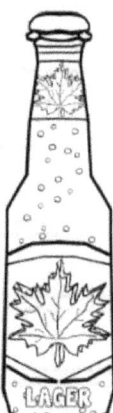

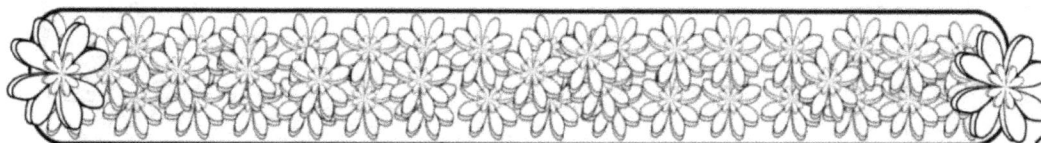

FML   Piss Off

129

Bride
Fuck Me

Notes
Checklist

Ray of Sunshine, GTFO

Groom
Fuck Me

Notes
Checklist

Ray of Sunshine, GTFO

131

Maid of Honour

Notes
Checklist

Today I Choose Happiness, FYFI

132

Bridesmaids Bitches

Notes Checklist

♥ _____ ♥ ♥ _____ ♥
♥ _____ ♥ ♥ _____ ♥
♥ _____ ♥ ♥ _____ ♥
♥ _____ ♥ ♥ _____ ♥
♥ _____ ♥ ♥ _____ ♥
♥ _____ ♥ ♥ _____ ♥
♥ _____ ♥ ♥ _____ ♥
♥ _____ ♥ ♥ _____ ♥
♥ _____ ♥ ♥ _____ ♥
♥ _____ ♥ ♥ _____ ♥
♥ _____ ♥ ♥ _____ ♥
♥ _____ ♥ ♥ _____ ♥

_____

_____

Love Yourself, Fuck Yes

Flower Girl Notes Checklist

Soulmate, OMFG

Ring Bearer

Notes Checklist

Enjoy Every Second, Bitch

Best Man Checklist

Notes

Be Patient, Kind, Fuck Yes

Groomsmen Checklist

Notes

Live, Love, Laugh, Fuck

Mother of Bride Checklist

Notes

Compromise, Kiss Ass

138

Father of Groom Checklist

Notes

Thank The Wedding Party, Shit Yes

Mother of Groom

Notes

Checklist

Believe in Magic, WTF, Yes

Father of Bride

Notes Checklist

Marriage, Lifelong, FYFI

141

Notes

Random Fucking Thoughts

Date:_____

Bitch Meter

Notes
Random Fucking Thoughts

Date: _____

Bitch Meter

Notes

Random Fucking Thoughts

Date: _____

Bitch Meter

144

Notes
Random Fucking Thoughts

Date: _____

Bitch Meter

Stay Hydrated

Date: _____

I Love Water, Drink up Bitch

146

Stay Hydrated

 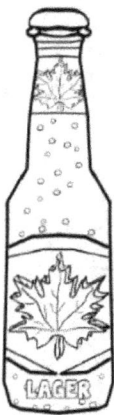     

FML   Piss Off

Stay Hydrated

Date:_____

I LoveWater, Drink up Bitch

Stay Hydrated

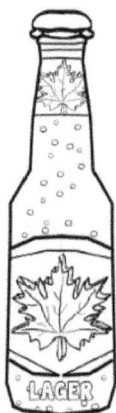 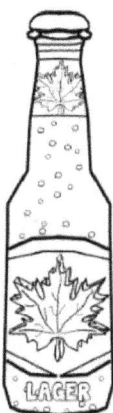 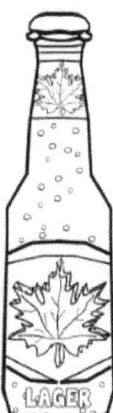   

FML   Piss Off

Month

Monday	Tuesday	Wednesday	Thursday
 ①②③④⑤	 ①②③④⑤	 ①②③④⑤	 ①②③④⑤
 ①②③④⑤	 ①②③④⑤	 ①②③④⑤	 ①②③④⑤
 ①②③④⑤	 ①②③④⑤	 ①②③④⑤	 ①②③④⑤
 ①②③④⑤	 ①②③④⑤	 ①②③④⑤	 ①②③④⑤
 ①②③④⑤	 ①②③④⑤	 ①②③④⑤	 ①②③④⑤

 Happy Happy Level ① ② ③ ④ ⑤   Anxiety Level ① ② ③ ④ ⑤

Friday	Saturday	Sunday	Notes
① ② ③ ④ ⑤	① ② ③ ④ ⑤	① ② ③ ④ ⑤	---------------
① ② ③ ④ ⑤	① ② ③ ④ ⑤	① ② ③ ④ ⑤	
① ② ③ ④ ⑤	① ② ③ ④ ⑤	① ② ③ ④ ⑤	
① ② ③ ④ ⑤	① ② ③ ④ ⑤	① ② ③ ④ ⑤	
① ② ③ ④ ⑤	① ② ③ ④ ⑤	① ② ③ ④ ⑤	

Note to Self

◇ Wedding Jitters   ♡ Time to be Happy is Today

☐ Love Yourself   ☆ You Got This

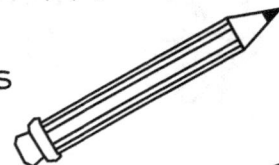

151

Month

Monday	Tuesday	Wednesday	Thursday
 ①②③④⑤	 ①②③④⑤	①②③④⑤	 ①②③④⑤
①②③④⑤	①②③④⑤	 ①②③④⑤	 ①②③④⑤
 ①②③④⑤	 ①②③④⑤	 ①②③④⑤	 ①②③④⑤
 ①②③④⑤	 ①②③④⑤	 ①②③④⑤	 ①②③④⑤
 ①②③④⑤	 ①②③④⑤	 ①②③④⑤	 ①②③④⑤

152

 Happy Happy Level ①②③④⑤  Anxiety Level ①②③④⑤

Friday	Saturday	Sunday	Notes
①②③④⑤	①②③④⑤	①②③④⑤	
①②③④⑤	①②③④⑤	①②③④⑤	
①②③④⑤	①②③④⑤	①②③④⑤	
①②③④⑤	①②③④⑤	①②③④⑤	
①②③④⑤	①②③④⑤	①②③④⑤	

Note to Self

◇ Wedding Jitters ♡ Time to be Happy is Today

☐ Love Yourself ☆ You Got This

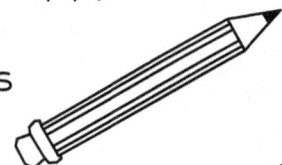

Month

Monday	Tuesday	Wednesday	Thursday
 ① 2 ③ 4 ⑤	 ① 2 ③ 4 ⑤	 ① 2 ③ 4 ⑤	 ① 2 ③ 4 ⑤
 ① 2 ③ 4 ⑤	 ① 2 ③ 4 ⑤	 ① 2 ③ 4 ⑤	 ① 2 ③ 4 ⑤
 ① 2 ③ 4 ⑤	 ① 2 ③ 4 ⑤	 ① 2 ③ 4 ⑤	 ① 2 ③ 4 ⑤
 ① 2 ③ 4 ⑤	 ① 2 ③ 4 ⑤	 ① 2 ③ 4 ⑤	 ① 2 ③ 4 ⑤
 ① 2 ③ 4 ⑤	 ① 2 ③ 4 ⑤	 ① 2 ③ 4 ⑤	 ① 2 ③ 4 ⑤

Happy Happy Level ① ② ③ ④ ⑤   Anxiety Level ① ② ③ ④ ⑤

Friday	Saturday	Sunday	Notes
① ② ③ ④ ⑤	① ② ③ ④ ⑤	① ② ③ ④ ⑤	-------------
① ② ③ ④ ⑤	① ② ③ ④ ⑤	① ② ③ ④ ⑤	
① ② ③ ④ ⑤	① ② ③ ④ ⑤	① ② ③ ④ ⑤	
① ② ③ ④ ⑤	① ② ③ ④ ⑤	① ② ③ ④ ⑤	
① ② ③ ④ ⑤	① ② ③ ④ ⑤	① ② ③ ④ ⑤	

Note to Self

◇ Wedding Jitters   ♡ Time to be Happy is Today

▢ Love Yourself   ☆ You Got This

155

Month

Monday	Tuesday	Wednesday	Thursday
 ①②③④⑤	 ①②③④⑤	 ①②③④⑤	 ①②③④⑤
 ①②③④⑤	 ①②③④⑤	 ①②③④⑤	 ①②③④⑤
 ①②③④⑤	 ①②③④⑤	 ①②③④⑤	 ①②③④⑤
 ①②③④⑤	 ①②③④⑤	 ①②③④⑤	 ①②③④⑤
 ①②③④⑤	 ①②③④⑤	 ①②③④⑤	 ①②③④⑤

Happy Happy Level ①②③④⑤   Anxiety Level ①②③④⑤

Friday	Saturday	Sunday	Notes
①②③④⑤	①②③④⑤	①②③④⑤	-------
①②③④⑤	①②③④⑤	①②③④⑤	
①②③④⑤	①②③④⑤	①②③④⑤	
①②③④⑤	①②③④⑤	①②③④⑤	
①②③④⑤	①②③④⑤	①②③④⑤	

Note to Self

◇ Wedding Jitters   ♡ Time to be Happy is Today

▢ Love Yourself   ☆ You Got This

Month

Monday	Tuesday	Wednesday	Thursday
 ① ② ③ ④ ⑤	 ① ② ③ ④ ⑤	① ② ③ ④ ⑤	 ① ② ③ ④ ⑤
 ① ② ③ ④ ⑤	① ② ③ ④ ⑤	 ① ② ③ ④ ⑤	 ① ② ③ ④ ⑤
 ① ② ③ ④ ⑤	 ① ② ③ ④ ⑤	 ① ② ③ ④ ⑤	 ① ② ③ ④ ⑤
 ① ② ③ ④ ⑤	 ① ② ③ ④ ⑤	 ① ② ③ ④ ⑤	 ① ② ③ ④ ⑤
 ① ② ③ ④ ⑤	 ① ② ③ ④ ⑤	 ① ② ③ ④ ⑤	 ① ② ③ ④ ⑤

Happy Happy Level ① ② ③ ④ ⑤   Anxiety Level ① ② ③ ④ ⑤

Friday	Saturday	Sunday	Notes
① ② ③ ④ ⑤	① ② ③ ④ ⑤	① ② ③ ④ ⑤	
① ② ③ ④ ⑤	① ② ③ ④ ⑤	① ② ③ ④ ⑤	
① ② ③ ④ ⑤	① ② ③ ④ ⑤	① ② ③ ④ ⑤	
① ② ③ ④ ⑤	① ② ③ ④ ⑤	① ② ③ ④ ⑤	
① ② ③ ④ ⑤	① ② ③ ④ ⑤	① ② ③ ④ ⑤	

Note to Self

◇ Wedding Jitters   ♡ Time to be Happy is Today

☐ Love Yourself   ☆ You Got This

159

Month

Monday	Tuesday	Wednesday	Thursday
 ①②③④⑤	 ①②③④⑤	 ①②③④⑤	 ①②③④⑤
 ①②③④⑤	 ①②③④⑤	 ①②③④⑤	 ①②③④⑤
 ①②③④⑤	 ①②③④⑤	 ①②③④⑤	 ①②③④⑤
 ①②③④⑤	 ①②③④⑤	 ①②③④⑤	 ①②③④⑤
 ①②③④⑤	 ①②③④⑤	 ①②③④⑤	 ①②③④⑤

160

 Happy Happy Level ①②③④⑤  Anxiety Level ①②③④⑤

Friday	Saturday	Sunday	Notes
 ①②③④⑤	 ①②③④⑤	 ①②③④⑤	‑‑‑‑‑‑‑‑‑‑
 ①②③④⑤	 ①②③④⑤	 ①②③④⑤	‑‑‑‑‑‑‑‑‑‑
 ①②③④⑤	 ①②③④⑤	 ①②③④⑤	‑‑‑‑‑‑‑‑‑‑
 ①②③④⑤	 ①②③④⑤	 ①②③④⑤	‑‑‑‑‑‑‑‑‑‑
 ①②③④⑤	 ①②③④⑤	 ①②③④⑤	‑‑‑‑‑‑‑‑‑‑

Note to Self

◇ Wedding Jitters   ♡ Time to be Happy is Today

▢ Love Yourself   ☆ You Got This

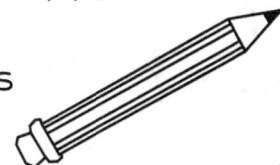

Month

Monday	Tuesday	Wednesday	Thursday
 ①②③④⑤	 ①②③④⑤	 ①②③④⑤	 ①②③④⑤
 ①②③④⑤	 ①②③④⑤	 ①②③④⑤	 ①②③④⑤
 ①②③④⑤	 ①②③④⑤	 ①②③④⑤	 ①②③④⑤
 ①②③④⑤	 ①②③④⑤	 ①②③④⑤	 ①②③④⑤
 ①②③④⑤	 ①②③④⑤	 ①②③④⑤	 ①②③④⑤

162

 Happy Happy Level ①②③④⑤  Anxiety Level ①②③④⑤

Friday	Saturday	Sunday	Notes
①②③④⑤	①②③④⑤	①②③④⑤	
①②③④⑤	①②③④⑤	①②③④⑤	
①②③④⑤	①②③④⑤	①②③④⑤	
①②③④⑤	①②③④⑤	①②③④⑤	
①②③④⑤	①②③④⑤	①②③④⑤	

Note to Self

◇ Wedding Jitters   ♡ Time to be Happy is Today

▢ Love Yourself   ☆ You Got This

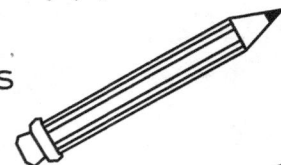

163

Month

Monday	Tuesday	Wednesday	Thursday
 ①②③④⑤	 ①②③④⑤	①②③④⑤	 ①②③④⑤
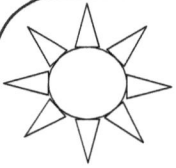 ①②③④⑤	①②③④⑤	①②③④⑤	①②③④⑤
①②③④⑤	 ①②③④⑤	①②③④⑤	①②③④⑤
①②③④⑤	①②③④⑤	①②③④⑤	①②③④⑤
①②③④⑤	①②③④⑤	①②③④⑤	①②③④⑤

Happy Happy Level ① ② ③ ④ ⑤   Anxiety Level ① ② ③ ④ ⑤

Friday	Saturday	Sunday	Notes
① ② ③ ④ ⑤	① ② ③ ④ ⑤	① ② ③ ④ ⑤	-------
① ② ③ ④ ⑤	① ② ③ ④ ⑤	① ② ③ ④ ⑤	-------
① ② ③ ④ ⑤	① ② ③ ④ ⑤	① ② ③ ④ ⑤	-------
① ② ③ ④ ⑤	① ② ③ ④ ⑤	① ② ③ ④ ⑤	-------
① ② ③ ④ ⑤	① ② ③ ④ ⑤	① ② ③ ④ ⑤	-------

Note to Self

◇ Wedding Jitters   ♡ Time to be Happy is Today

▢ Love Yourself   ☆ You Got This

165

Month

Monday	Tuesday	Wednesday	Thursday
 ①②③④⑤	 ①②③④⑤	①②③④⑤	 ①②③④⑤
 ①②③④⑤	 ①②③④⑤	 ①②③④⑤	①②③④⑤
 ①②③④⑤	 ①②③④⑤	 ①②③④⑤	①②③④⑤
 ①②③④⑤	 ①②③④⑤	 ①②③④⑤	①②③④⑤
①②③④⑤	 ①②③④⑤	①②③④⑤	 ①②③④⑤

166

Friday	Saturday	Sunday	Notes

① ② ③ ④ ⑤   ① ② ③ ④ ⑤   ① ② ③ ④ ⑤

① ② ③ ④ ⑤   ① ② ③ ④ ⑤   ① ② ③ ④ ⑤

① ② ③ ④ ⑤   ① ② ③ ④ ⑤   ① ② ③ ④ ⑤

① ② ③ ④ ⑤   ① ② ③ ④ ⑤   ① ② ③ ④ ⑤

① ② ③ ④ ⑤   ① ② ③ ④ ⑤   ① ② ③ ④ ⑤

Note to Self

◇ Wedding Jitters   ♡ Time to be Happy is Today

▢ Love Yourself   ☆ You Got This

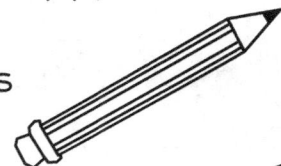

167

Month

Monday	Tuesday	Wednesday	Thursday
① ② ③ ④ ⑤	① ② ③ ④ ⑤	① ② ③ ④ ⑤	① ② ③ ④ ⑤
① ② ③ ④ ⑤	① ② ③ ④ ⑤	① ② ③ ④ ⑤	① ② ③ ④ ⑤
① ② ③ ④ ⑤	① ② ③ ④ ⑤	① ② ③ ④ ⑤	① ② ③ ④ ⑤
① ② ③ ④ ⑤	① ② ③ ④ ⑤	① ② ③ ④ ⑤	① ② ③ ④ ⑤
① ② ③ ④ ⑤	① ② ③ ④ ⑤	① ② ③ ④ ⑤	① ② ③ ④ ⑤

Happy Happy Level ① ② ③ ④ ⑤ Anxiety Level ① ② ③ ④ ⑤

Friday	Saturday	Sunday	Notes

① ② ③ ④ ⑤

① ② ③ ④ ⑤

① ② ③ ④ ⑤

————————————
————————————
————————————
————————————

① ② ③ ④ ⑤

① ② ③ ④ ⑤

① ② ③ ④ ⑤

————————————
————————————
————————————
————————————

① ② ③ ④ ⑤

① ② ③ ④ ⑤

① ② ③ ④ ⑤

————————————
————————————
————————————
————————————

① ② ③ ④ ⑤

① ② ③ ④ ⑤

① ② ③ ④ ⑤

————————————
————————————
————————————
————————————

① ② ③ ④ ⑤

① ② ③ ④ ⑤

① ② ③ ④ ⑤

————————————
————————————
————————————

Note to Self

◇ Wedding Jitters   ♡ Time to be Happy is Today

▢ Love Yourself   ☆ You Got This

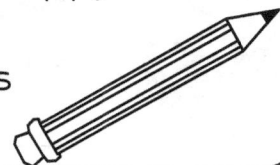

Month

Monday	Tuesday	Wednesday	Thursday
① ② ③ ④ ⑤	① ② ③ ④ ⑤	① ② ③ ④ ⑤	① ② ③ ④ ⑤
① ② ③ ④ ⑤	① ② ③ ④ ⑤	① ② ③ ④ ⑤	① ② ③ ④ ⑤
① ② ③ ④ ⑤	① ② ③ ④ ⑤	① ② ③ ④ ⑤	① ② ③ ④ ⑤
① ② ③ ④ ⑤	① ② ③ ④ ⑤	① ② ③ ④ ⑤	① ② ③ ④ ⑤
① ② ③ ④ ⑤	① ② ③ ④ ⑤	① ② ③ ④ ⑤	① ② ③ ④ ⑤

170

Happy Happy Level

Happy Happy Level ① ② ③ ④ ⑤  Anxiety Level ① ② ③ ④ ⑤

Friday	Saturday	Sunday	Notes
① ② ③ ④ ⑤	① ② ③ ④ ⑤	① ② ③ ④ ⑤	
① ② ③ ④ ⑤	① ② ③ ④ ⑤	① ② ③ ④ ⑤	
① ② ③ ④ ⑤	① ② ③ ④ ⑤	① ② ③ ④ ⑤	
① ② ③ ④ ⑤	① ② ③ ④ ⑤	① ② ③ ④ ⑤	
① ② ③ ④ ⑤	① ② ③ ④ ⑤	① ② ③ ④ ⑤	

Note to Self

◇ Wedding Jitters   ♡ Time to be Happy is Today

▢ Love Yourself   ☆ You Got This

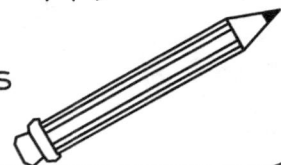

171

Month

Monday	Tuesday	Wednesday	Thursday
① ② ③ ④ ⑤	① ② ③ ④ ⑤	① ② ③ ④ ⑤	① ② ③ ④ ⑤
① ② ③ ④ ⑤	① ② ③ ④ ⑤	① ② ③ ④ ⑤	① ② ③ ④ ⑤
① ② ③ ④ ⑤	① ② ③ ④ ⑤	① ② ③ ④ ⑤	① ② ③ ④ ⑤
① ② ③ ④ ⑤	① ② ③ ④ ⑤	① ② ③ ④ ⑤	① ② ③ ④ ⑤
① ② ③ ④ ⑤	① ② ③ ④ ⑤	① ② ③ ④ ⑤	① ② ③ ④ ⑤

172

Happy Happy Level ① ② ③ ④ ⑤

Anxiety Level ① ② ③ ④ ⑤

Friday	Saturday	Sunday	Notes
 ① ② ③ ④ ⑤	 ① ② ③ ④ ⑤	① ② ③ ④ ⑤	
① ② ③ ④ ⑤	① ② ③ ④ ⑤	① ② ③ ④ ⑤	
① ② ③ ④ ⑤	① ② ③ ④ ⑤	 ① ② ③ ④ ⑤	
① ② ③ ④ ⑤	 ① ② ③ ④ ⑤	 ① ② ③ ④ ⑤	
 ① ② ③ ④ ⑤	 ① ② ③ ④ ⑤	① ② ③ ④ ⑤	

Note to Self

◇ Wedding Jitters   ♡ Time to be Happy is Today

▢ Love Yourself   ☆ You Got This

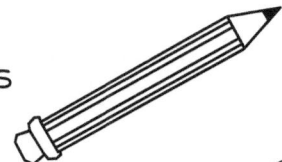

Random Fucking Thoughts

Bitch Meter

Notes
Random Fucking Thoughts

Date:

Bitch Meter

Notes
Random Fucking Thoughts

Bitch Meter

Notes
Random Fucking Thoughts

Date:_____

Bitch Meter

Weekly Planner

Mon _____
_____

Bitch Meter

☆ ☆ ☆ ☆

Tues _____
_____

Hydrated

Wed _____
_____

Thur _____
_____

Fri _____
_____

Sat _____
_____

Sun _____
_____

178

# Weekly Planner

Bitch Meter

☆ ☆ ☆ ☆

Mon _____
_____

Tues _____
_____

Wed _____
_____

## Hydrated

Thur _____
_____

Fri _____
_____

Sat _____
_____

Sun _____
_____

Date: _____

Weekly Planner

Date: _____

Mon _____

Tues _____

Wed _____

Thur _____

Fri _____

Sat _____

Sun _____

Bitch Meter

☆ ☆ ☆ ☆

Hydrated

Weekly Planner

Mon _____

Tues _____

Wed _____

Thur _____

Fri _____

Sat _____

Sun _____

Bitch Meter

☆ ☆ ☆ ☆

Hydrated

181

Weekly Planner

Date: _____

Bitch Meter

☆ ☆ ☆ ☆

Hydrated

Mon _____

Tues _____

Wed _____

Thur _____

Fri _____

Sat _____

Sun _____

182

Weekly Planner

Bitch Meter

☆ ☆ ☆ ☆

Hydrated

Date: _____

Mon _____

Tues _____

Wed _____

Thur _____

Fri _____

Sat _____

Sun _____

Date: _____

Weekly Planner

Bitch Meter

☆ ☆ ☆ ☆

Hydrated

Mon _____

Tues _____

Wed _____

Thur _____

Fri _____

Sat _____

Sun _____

184

Weekly Planner

Date: _____

Mon
_____
_____
_____

Tues
_____
_____
_____

Wed
_____
_____
_____

Thur
_____
_____
_____

Fri
_____
_____
_____

Sat
_____
_____
_____

Sun
_____
_____

Bitch Meter

☆ ☆ ☆ ☆

Hydrated

Weekly Planner

Date: _____

Mon
_____
_____

Tues
_____
_____

Wed
_____
_____

Thur
_____
_____

Fri
_____
_____

Sat
_____
_____

Sun
_____
_____

Bitch Meter

☆ ☆ ☆ ☆

Hydrated

186

Weekly Planner

Bitch Meter

☆ ☆ ☆ ☆

Hydrated

Date: _____

Mon _____
✿ _____

Tues _____
✿ _____

Wed _____
✿ _____

Thur _____
✿ _____

Fri _____
✿ _____

Sat _____
✿ _____

Sun _____
✿ _____

187

Weekly Planner

Date: _____

Bitch Meter

☆ ☆ ☆ ☆

Hydrated

Mon
_____
_____

Tues
_____
_____

Wed
_____
_____

Thur
_____
_____

Fri
_____
_____

Sat
_____
_____

Sun
_____
_____

188

Weekly Planner

Date: _____

Mon _____
_____

Tues _____
_____

Wed _____
_____

Thur _____
_____

Fri _____
_____

Sat _____
_____

Sun _____
_____

Bitch Meter

☆ ☆ ☆ ☆

Hydrated

189

Weekly Planner

Date: _____

Bitch Meter

☆ ☆ ☆ ☆

Hydrated

Mon _____
_____

Tues _____
_____

Wed _____
_____

Thur _____
_____

Fri _____
_____

Sat _____
_____

Sun _____
_____

190

Weekly Planner

Date: _____

Mon _____

Tues _____

Wed _____

Thur _____

Fri _____

Sat _____

Sun _____

Bitch Meter

☆ ☆ ☆ ☆

Hydrated

191

Weekly Planner

Date: _____

Mon _____

Tues _____

Wed _____

Thur _____

Fri _____

Sat _____

Sun _____

Bitch Meter

☆ ☆ ☆ ☆

Hydrated

Weekly Planner

Mon _____
_____
_____

Tues _____
_____
_____

Wed _____
_____
_____

Thur _____
_____
_____

Fri _____
_____
_____

Sat _____
_____
_____

Sun _____
_____
_____

Bitch Meter

☆ ☆ ☆ ☆

Hydrated

193

 # Weekly Planner

Date: _____

Bitch Meter

☆ ☆ ☆ ☆

Hydrated

Mon _____

Tues _____

Wed _____

Thur _____

Fri _____

Sat _____

Sun _____

194

Weekly Planner

Bitch Meter

☆ ☆ ☆ ☆

Mon

Tues

Wed

Hydrated

Thur

Fri

Sat

Sun

Weekly Planner

Bitch Meter

☆ ☆ ☆ ☆

Hydrated

Mon _____

Tues _____

Wed _____

Thur _____

Fri _____

Sat _____

Sun _____

Weekly Planner

Date: _____

Bitch Meter

☆ ☆ ☆ ☆

Hydrated

Mon _____

Tues _____

Wed _____

Thur _____

Fri _____

Sat _____

Sun _____

Weekly Planner

Bitch Meter

☆ ☆ ☆ ☆

Hydrated

Mon

Tues

Wed

Thur

Fri

Sat

Sun

Weekly Planner

Bitch Meter

☆ ☆ ☆ ☆

Mon _____
_____

Tues _____
_____

Wed _____
_____

Hydrated

Thur _____
_____

Fri _____
_____

Sat _____
_____

Sun _____
_____

199

Weekly Planner

Mon _____
_____

Tues _____
_____

Wed _____
_____

Thur _____
_____

Fri _____
_____

Sat _____
_____

Sun _____
_____

Bitch Meter

☆ ☆ ☆ ☆

Hydrated

200

Weekly Planner

Date: _____

Mon _____
_____

Bitch Meter

☆ ☆ ☆ ☆

Tues _____
_____

Hydrated

Wed _____
_____

Thur _____
_____

Fri _____
_____

Sat _____
_____

Sun _____
_____

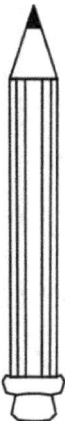

Weekly Planner

Mon ————————————
————————————
————————————

Bitch Meter

☆ ☆ ☆ ☆

Tues ————————————
————————————
————————————

Wed ————————————
————————————
————————————

Hydrated

Thur ————————————
————————————
————————————

Fri ————————————
————————————
————————————

← → ← → ← → ← → ← → ← → ← → ← → ← → ← →

Sat ————————————
————————————
————————————

Sun ————————————
————————————
————————————

202

Weekly Planner

Date: _____

Mon
_____
_____
_____

Tues
_____
_____
_____

Wed
_____
_____
_____

Thur
_____
_____
_____

Fri
_____
_____
_____

Sat
_____
_____
_____

Sun
_____
_____
_____

Bitch Meter

☆ ☆ ☆ ☆

Hydrated

203

Weekly Planner

Date: _____

Bitch Meter

☆ ☆ ☆ ☆

Hydrated

Mon _____

Tues _____

Wed _____

Thur _____

Fri _____

Sat _____

Sun _____

204

Weekly Planner

Date: _____

Mon _____

Tues _____

Wed _____

Thur _____

Fri _____

Sat _____

Sun _____

Bitch Meter

☆ ☆ ☆ ☆

Hydrated

Weekly Planner

Date: _____

Mon _____
_____

Tues _____
_____

Wed _____
_____

Thur _____
_____

Fri _____
_____

Sat _____
_____

Sun _____
_____

Bitch Meter

☆ ☆ ☆ ☆

Hydrated

206

Weekly Planner

Mon _____

Tues _____

Wed _____

Thur _____

Fri _____

Sat _____

Sun _____

Bitch Meter

☆ ☆ ☆ ☆

Hydrated

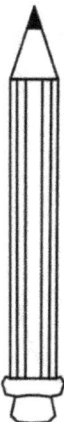

 # Weekly Planner

Bitch Meter

☆ ☆ ☆ ☆

Hydrated

Mon _____

Tues _____

Wed _____

Thur _____

Fri _____

Sat _____

Sun _____

 # Weekly Planner

Bitch Meter

☆ ☆ ☆ ☆

Hydrated

Mon _____

Tues _____

Wed _____

Thur _____

Fri _____

Sat _____

Sun _____

Notes
Random Fucking Thoughts

Date: _____

Bitch Meter

Water Water Water Water Water Water Water Water Water

Water Water Water Water Water Water Water Water Water

Notes

Random Fucking Thoughts

Date: _____

Bitch Meter

211

Notes
Random Fucking Thoughts

Date: _____

Bitch Meter

Notes
Random Fucking Thoughts

Date: _____

Bitch Meter

Health Tracker

Workout   Water

Mon
Breakfast _____
Lunch _____
Dinner _____

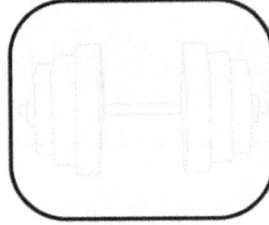

Tues
Breakfast _____
Lunch _____
Dinner _____

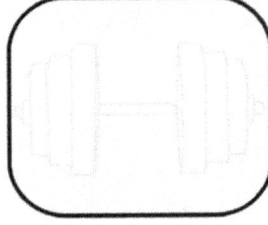

Wed
Breakfast _____
Lunch _____
Dinner _____

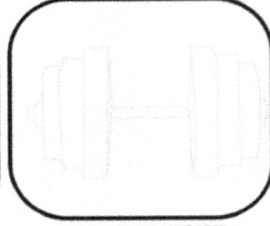

Thur
Breakfast _____
Lunch _____
Dinner _____

Fri
Breakfast _____
Lunch _____
Dinner _____

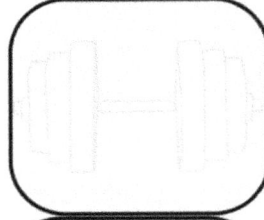

Sat
Breakfast _____
Lunch _____
Dinner _____

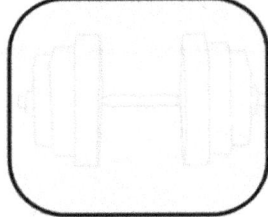

Sun
Breakfast _____
Lunch _____
Dinner _____

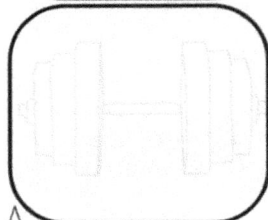

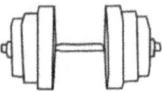

Energy Level

214

Health Tracker

Workout　**Water**

Mon
Breakfast _____
Lunch _____
Dinner _____

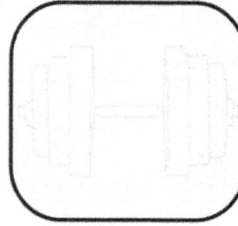 

Tues
Breakfast _____
Lunch _____
Dinner _____

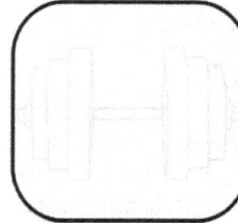 

Wed
Breakfast _____
Lunch _____
Dinner _____

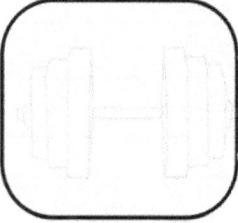 

Thur
Breakfast _____
Lunch _____
Dinner _____

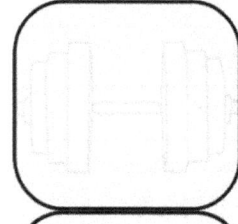 

Fri
Breakfast _____
Lunch _____
Dinner _____

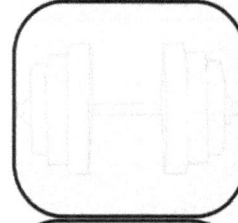 

Sat
Breakfast _____
Lunch _____
Dinner _____

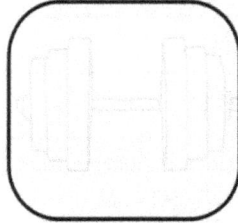 

Sun
Breakfast _____
Lunch _____
Dinner _____

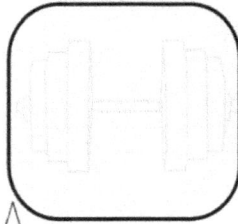 

 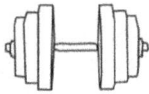 

Energy Level

215

Health Tracker

Workout **Water**

Mon
Breakfast _____
Lunch _____
Dinner _____

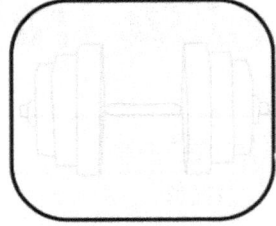 

Tues
Breakfast _____
Lunch _____
Dinner _____

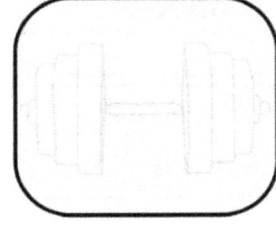 

Wed
Breakfast _____
Lunch _____
Dinner _____

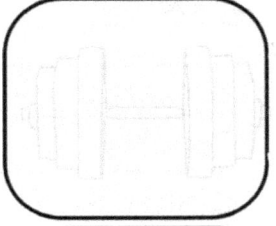 

Thur
Breakfast _____
Lunch _____
Dinner _____

Fri
Breakfast _____
Lunch _____
Dinner _____

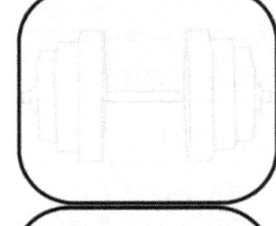 

Sat
Breakfast _____
Lunch _____
Dinner _____

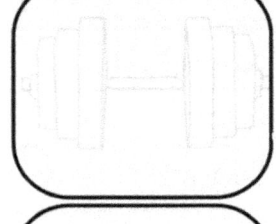 

Sun
Breakfast _____
Lunch _____
Dinner _____

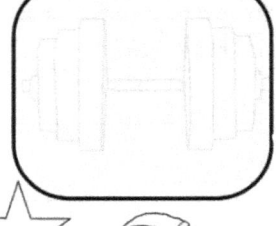 

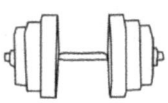

Energy Level

Health Tracker

Workout   **Water**

Mon
Breakfast _____
Lunch _____
Dinner _____

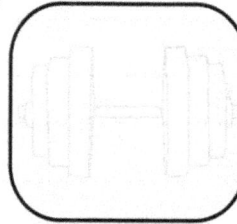

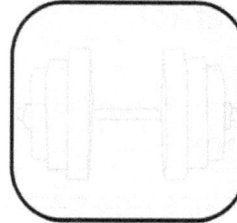

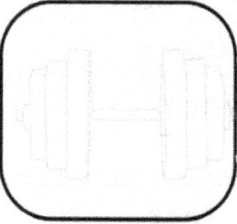

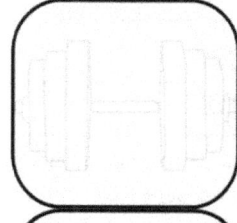

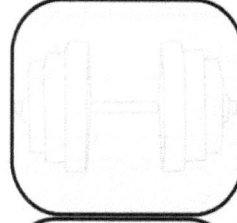

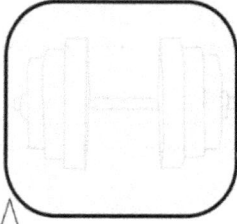

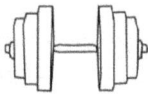

Tues
Breakfast _____
Lunch _____
Dinner _____

Wed
Breakfast _____
Lunch _____
Dinner _____

Thur
Breakfast _____
Lunch _____
Dinner _____

Fri
Breakfast _____
Lunch _____
Dinner _____

Sat
Breakfast _____
Lunch _____
Dinner _____

Sun
Breakfast _____
Lunch _____
Dinner _____

Energy Level

217

# Health Tracker

Workout　　**Water**

Mon
- **Breakfast** _____
- **Lunch** _____
- **Dinner** _____

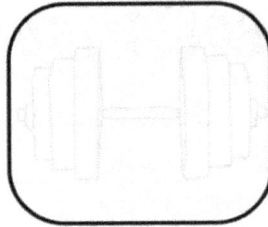 

Tues
- **Breakfast** _____
- **Lunch** _____
- **Dinner** _____

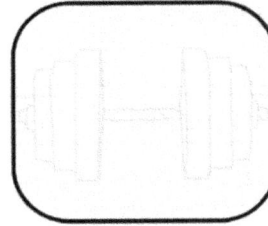 

Wed
- **Breakfast** _____
- **Lunch** _____
- **Dinner** _____

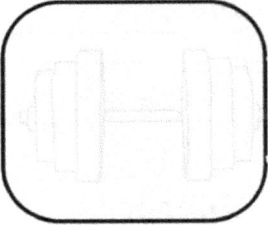 

Thur
- **Breakfast** _____
- **Lunch** _____
- **Dinner** _____

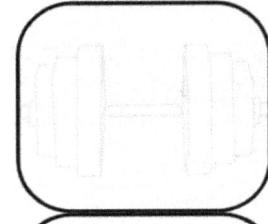 

Fri
- **Breakfast** _____
- **Lunch** _____
- **Dinner** _____

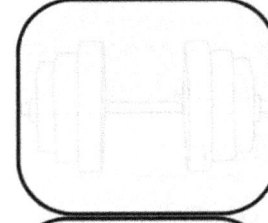 

Sat
- **Breakfast** _____
- **Lunch** _____
- **Dinner** _____

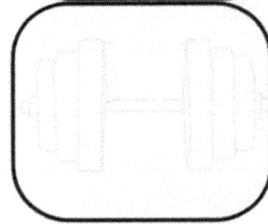 

Sun
- **Breakfast** _____
- **Lunch** _____
- **Dinner** _____

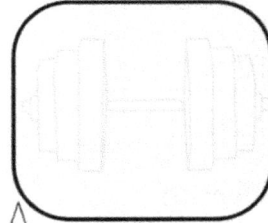 

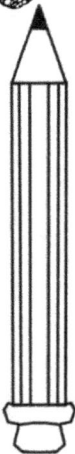
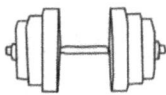

Energy Level

Health Tracker

Workout   **Water**

Date: _____

Mon
Breakfast _____
Lunch _____
Dinner _____

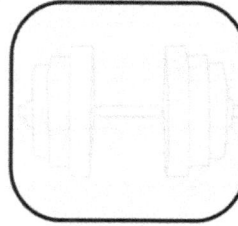

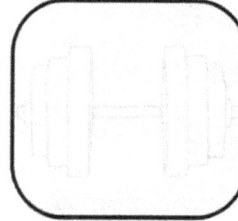

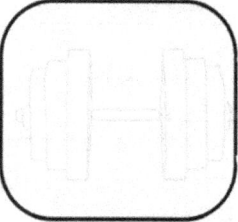

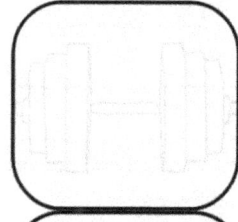

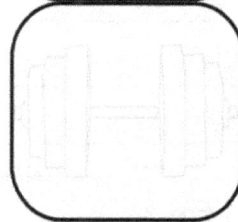

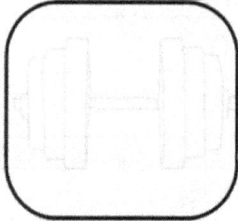

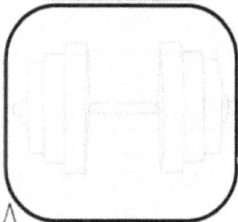

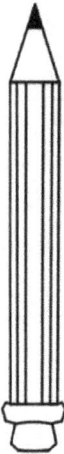

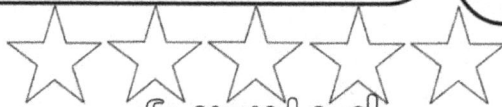

Tues
Breakfast _____
Lunch _____
Dinner _____

Wed
Breakfast _____
Lunch _____
Dinner _____

Thur
Breakfast _____
Lunch _____
Dinner _____

Fri
Breakfast _____
Lunch _____
Dinner _____

Sat
Breakfast _____
Lunch _____
Dinner _____

Sun
Breakfast _____
Lunch _____
Dinner _____

Energy Level

219

Health Tracker

Date: _____

Workout   Water

Mon
Breakfast _____
Lunch _____
Dinner _____
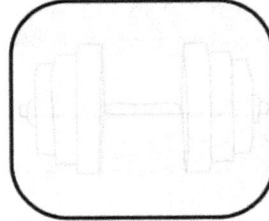

Tues
Breakfast _____
Lunch _____
Dinner _____
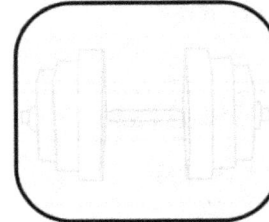

Wed
Breakfast _____
Lunch _____
Dinner _____
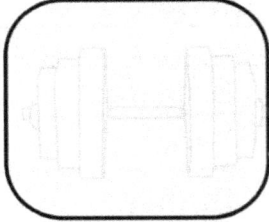

Thur
Breakfast _____
Lunch _____
Dinner _____
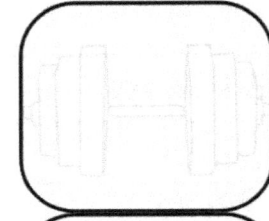

Fri
Breakfast _____
Lunch _____
Dinner _____
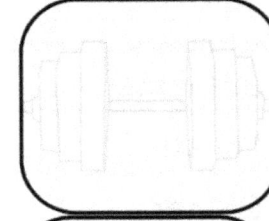

Sat
Breakfast _____
Lunch _____
Dinner _____
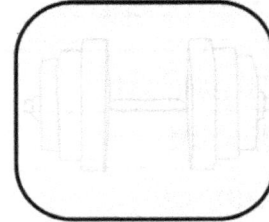

Sun
Breakfast _____
Lunch _____
Dinner _____
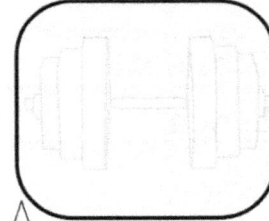

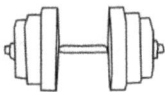

Energy Level

Health Tracker

Workout **Water**

Mon
Breakfast _____
Lunch _____
Dinner _____

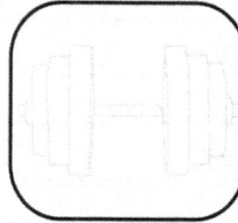

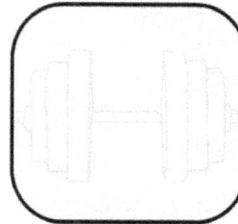

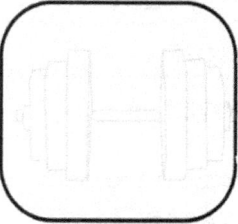

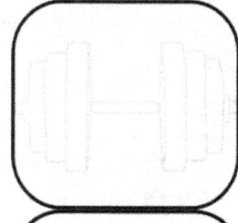

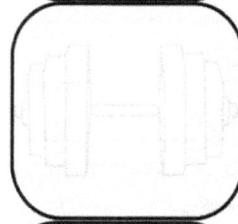

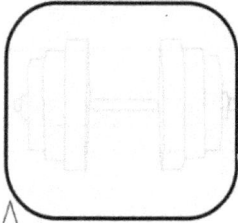

Tues
Breakfast _____
Lunch _____
Dinner _____

Wed
Breakfast _____
Lunch _____
Dinner _____

Thur
Breakfast _____
Lunch _____
Dinner _____

Fri
Breakfast _____
Lunch _____
Dinner _____

Sat
Breakfast _____
Lunch _____
Dinner _____

Sun
Breakfast _____
Lunch _____
Dinner _____

Energy Level

 # Health Tracker

Workout   **Date:** _____

Water

Mon
Breakfast _____
Lunch _____
Dinner _____
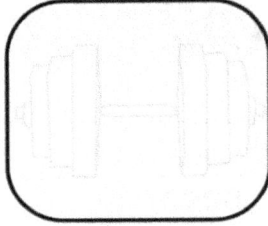 

Tues
Breakfast _____
Lunch _____
Dinner _____
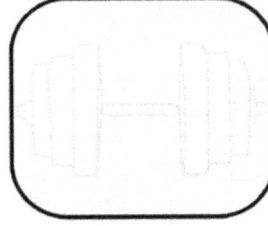 

Wed
Breakfast _____
Lunch _____
Dinner _____
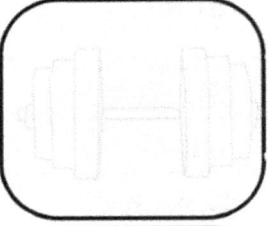 

Thur
Breakfast _____
Lunch _____
Dinner _____

Fri
Breakfast _____
Lunch _____
Dinner _____
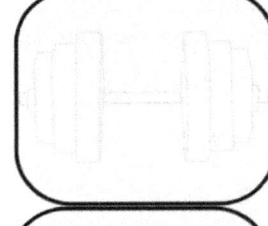 

Sat
Breakfast _____
Lunch _____
Dinner _____
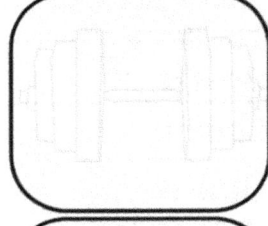 

Sun
Breakfast _____
Lunch _____
Dinner _____
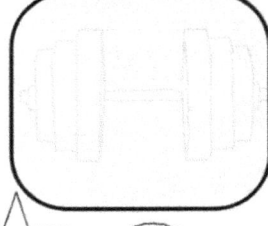 

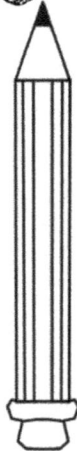 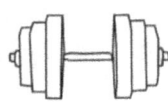  

Energy Level

 # Health Tracker   Workout   Water

Date: _____

Mon
Breakfast _____
Lunch _____
Dinner _____

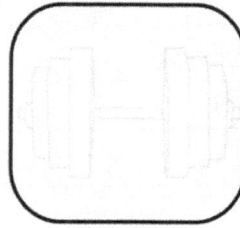 

Tues
Breakfast _____
Lunch _____
Dinner _____

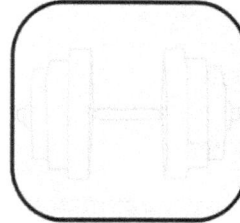 

Wed
Breakfast _____
Lunch _____
Dinner _____

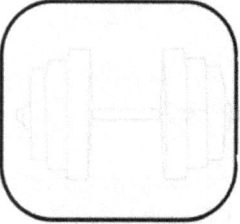 

Thur
Breakfast _____
Lunch _____
Dinner _____

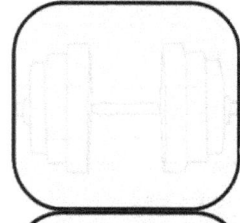 

Fri
Breakfast _____
Lunch _____
Dinner _____

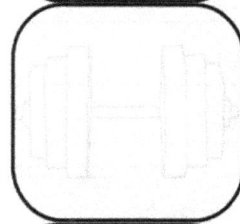 

Sat
Breakfast _____
Lunch _____
Dinner _____

Sun
Breakfast _____
Lunch _____
Dinner _____

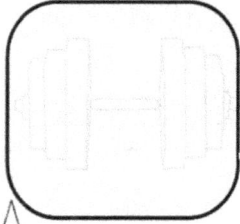 

 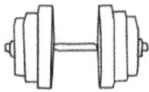 

Energy Level

 # Health Tracker

Workout Water

Mon
Breakfast _____
Lunch _____
Dinner _____

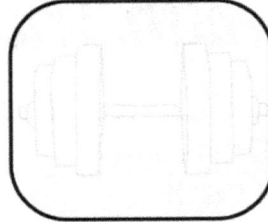 

Tues
Breakfast _____
Lunch _____
Dinner _____

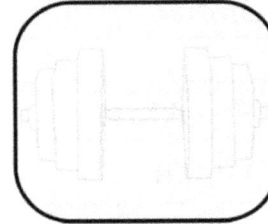 

Wed
Breakfast _____
Lunch _____
Dinner _____

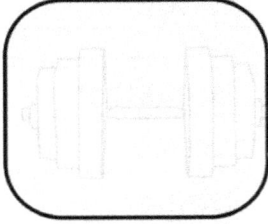 

Thur
Breakfast _____
Lunch _____
Dinner _____

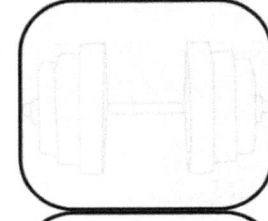 

Fri
Breakfast _____
Lunch _____
Dinner _____

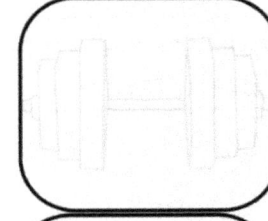 

Sat
Breakfast _____
Lunch _____
Dinner _____

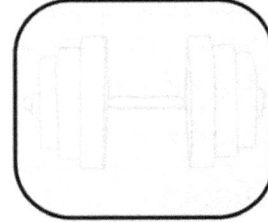 

Sun
Breakfast _____
Lunch _____
Dinner _____

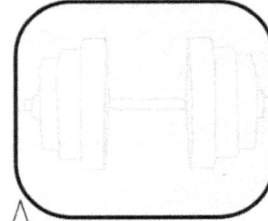 

  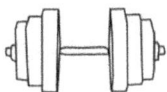  

Energy Level

Health Tracker

Workout   **Water**

Mon
Breakfast _____
Lunch _____
Dinner _____

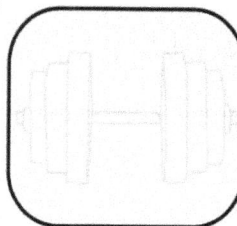

Tues
Breakfast _____
Lunch _____
Dinner _____

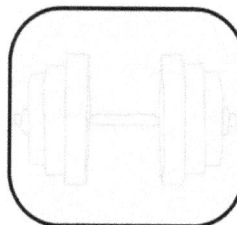

Wed
Breakfast _____
Lunch _____
Dinner _____

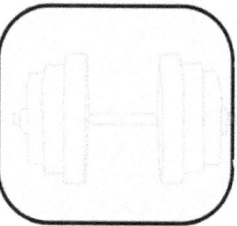

Thur
Breakfast _____
Lunch _____
Dinner _____

Fri
Breakfast _____
Lunch _____
Dinner _____

Sat
Breakfast _____
Lunch _____
Dinner _____

Sun
Breakfast _____
Lunch _____
Dinner _____

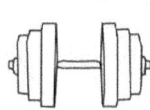

Energy Level

Notes
Random Fucking Thoughts

Date: _____

Bitch Meter

Water Water Water Water Water Water Water Water Water

Water Water Water Water Water Water Water Water Water

Notes
Random Fucking Thoughts

Date: _____

Bitch Meter

Notes
Random Fucking Thoughts

Date: _____

Bitch Meter

Water Water Water Water Water Water Water Water Water

Water Water Water Water Water Water Water Water Water

Notes

Date:———

Random Fucking Thoughts

Bitch Meter

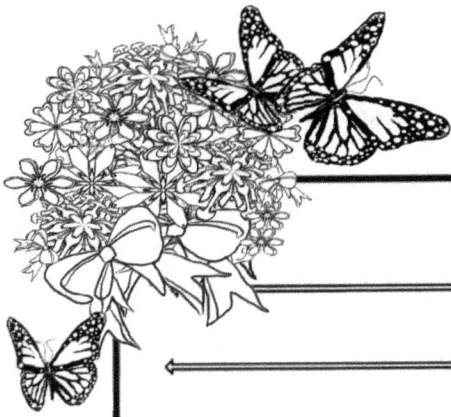

Date: _____

CALL OR TEXT, SHIT

Got This, Goals

Happy Happy

Kick Ass Notes

Habit Tracker

Be Thankful For

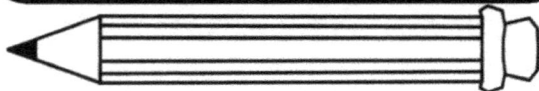

You Got This!

230

Call and Email

Free Time, Chill

ILP!

Today's Check List

Water Water Water Water Water

Mood Meter

LMM!

BLG!

Happy Day Tracker

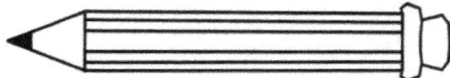

231

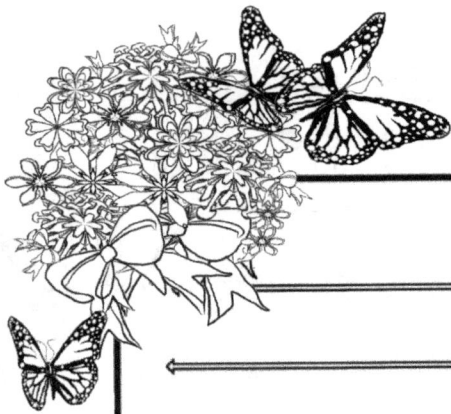

Date: _____

CALL OR TEXT, SHIT

Got This, Goals

Happy Happy

Kick Ass Notes

Habit Tracker

Be Thankful For

You Got This!

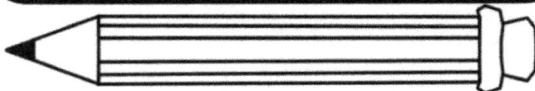

Call and Email

Date: _____
Mon Tues Wed Thur Fri Sat Sun

Free Time, Chill

ILY!

Today's Check List

Mood Meter

Happy Day Tracker

⭐⭐⭐⭐☆

Date: _____

CALL OR TEXT, SHIT

Got This, Goals
Happy Happy

Kick Ass Notes

Habit Tracker

Be Thankful For

You Got This!

 **Call and Email**

Free Time, Chill

UP!

Today's Check List

Mood Meter

LWL! ALG!

Happy Day Tracker

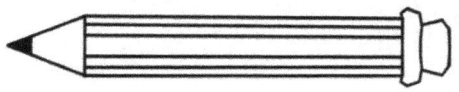

Date: _____

CALL OR TEXT, SHIT

Got This, Goals

Happy Happy

Kick Ass Notes

Habit Tracker

Be Thankful For

You Got This!

Call and Email

Free Time, Chill

ILY!

Today's Check List

Mood Meter

LML!   ALG!

Happy Day Tracker

237

Date: _____

CALL OR TEXT, SHIT

Got This, Goals

Happy Happy

Kick Ass Notes

Habit Tracker

Be Thankful For

You Got This!

238

✿ Call and Email

Free Time, Chill

ILY!

Today's Check List ✓

Mood Meter

LML! BLG!

Happy Day Tracker

☆ ☆ ☆ ☆ ☆

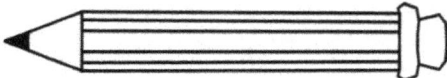

239

Thank You

By Mary Sweary   242

www.ingramcontent.com/pod-product-compliance
Lightning Source LLC
LaVergne TN
LVHW061334060426
835511LV00014B/1928

9 781988 097244